Phoenix Transforming

FROM ASHES TO ASCENSION

Lesa Butler

S.H.E. PUBLISHING, LLC

For information contact :
www.shepublishingllc.com
info@shepublishingllc.com

Lesa Butler - S.H.E. PUBLISHING, LLC
(shepublishingllc.com)

Cover and Title Page Design by :
Michelle Phillips of CHELLD3 3D
VISUALIZATION AND DESIGN

ISBN : 978-1-953163-44-8

First Edition : May 2022

10 9 8 7 6 5 4 3 2 1

Dedication

This book is dedicated to every villager who contributed to my ascension. To those who have been on the front lines of this battle with me for decades, THANK YOU! For those who have come in more recently and accepted the baton, THANK YOU! For every ounce of love, compassion, grace, and forgiveness afforded me, THANK YOU! For each sacrifice made on my behalf, THANK YOU! For every opportunity extended, THANK YOU!

THANK YOU!

THANK YOU!

THANK YOU!

Marissa, DeMares, and Maya,

You are the reason my wings have been set ablaze.

Love you forever and always.

Mama, you are poetry in motion.

Grandma, I hope I have made you proud.

Contents

"Healing is a process. It is not a one and done. We go through the metamorphosis from caterpillar to butterfly many times throughout our life's journey. And it's not about perfection, for that is an unreachable destination. The most desirable destination is to be perfect in our imperfection. Then we are perfectly changed."

~ LB

Imagine a creature so frighteningly beautiful that to behold it means the snatching away of your breath. Encapsulated by the light and heat of a raging fire, you are torn by two diametrically opposite inclinations: to reach out and touch it or turn and run away. Each choice has its risks and its rewards. If you step toward it, there is a chance that you will be drawn in and engulfed by the flames. Running away may leave you consumed with the question, "What if?" Either way, this magnificent, intriguing creature has left an indelible mark in your mind.

There is a legend featuring such a creature. This entity was called the Phoenix. It materialized in the form of a giant, fiery, dragon-like bird with a menacing, yet stunning presence. It invoked terror and awe simultaneously, leaving one in conflict regarding how to approach it, or to approach it at all. Every five hundred years, this mythical, magical bird would awaken from a deep slumber and begin its ascent toward the heavens in pursuit of its semi-millennial encounter with the sun.

The Phoenix was the soulmate to the sun. The sun awaited its arrival with sweet anticipation every five hundred years. Upon connection, the two did a lovemaking dance resulting in a transference of power, fire, and energy from star to bird. In that moment, no longer was the Phoenix average and commonplace, covered in the soot and ashes of its struggle. Immediately upon entrance into the vicinity of the power giver, it began to reflect the brilliance and awesomeness of the magnificent star. There was an awakening of magnani- mous proportions. The Phoenix was reborn.

Perhaps one of the most interesting parts of this story is the fact that the Phoenix began its journey from the ground. It started from a low place where it landed after the fire that had once covered it had fizzled out. When the designated time drew near, it got up slowly and awkwardly, beginning its ascent through the sky. Once the sun reset the Phoenix's fire, it soared through the heavens, lighting and heating everything in its path until the time came for it to take its rest again. After a 500-year period of rest, it rose again, repeating the cycle. This was the life of a Phoenix.

The legend of the Phoenix is comprised of multiple ideals and themes. One of the biggest is sacrifice. The Phoenix voluntarily allowed itself to be set on fire so that others could use its body for light and heat. It knew that it would become depleted and powerless, yet, it continued to arise. Even during the descent to the vulnerable place, anything in its path close enough to feel its presence received the benefit of whatever it still had left to give. Repeatedly, this selfless being flew upward, fully cognizant of what the outcome would be.

The legend of the Phoenix is also about transformation, hope, strength, and wisdom. Every five hundred years, it submitted to becoming a different, more empowered version of itself after resting in a space of weakness. The sun provided the hope and strength it needed to make the transformation. It was endowed with the wisdom to

> "The legend of the Phoenix is also about transformation, hope, strength, and wisdom."

know where, when, and how to access her life source. The journey of the rise of the Phoenix is an epic tale, one that has fascinated people for an exceptionally long time. I think you can understand why.

Do you see yourself in the Phoenix? I certainly do. I, too, have begun my ascent toward the sun from a place of rock bottom. I also awoke one day tired, disoriented, and covered in the ashes of my skirmishes with life. Like the Phoenix, I knew that I had to find my power source, or I would die, literally and figuratively. So, after a forced rest, I got up and began to feel my way through. After several attempts, I began to fly. The first couple of attempts were futile because I needed just a little more rest, and my wings were still being prepared. Oh, but over time, with grace and consistent effort, I was able to get off the ground inch by inch. Armed with endurance, resilience, and a quest for veracity at my side, I was soon in midair! Before I knew it, I was flying next to myself bearing witness to the pulchritude of this phenomenal poetry in motion. Rising with the cadence and rhythm of a well-orchestrated lyrical masterpiece, I commenced my approach toward the grand star that anxiously awaited the opportunity to reignite my fire. My resurrection was successful!

Do you know what I know about you? Your resurrection will be successful, too. No longer will you lie in the soot and ashes of your perceived failures, disappointments, or dysfunction. You WILL rise, you WILL soar, and you WILL be set ablaze! I am speaking directly to the Phoenix in you. Right now, you may be lying in dust and cinders, trying to gather the strength just to sit up. You have managed to get a few inches off the ground and are trying to get some lift. You could even be in full soar trying to go a little bit higher. Wherever you are in your journey, know that you will eventually reach the sun, and your wings will be set on fire. You will once again be an embodiment of light and heat for yourself, as well as those around you. You will LIVE and not die. Transformation is upon you!

I would like to invite you to accompany me on this flight toward the sun. In the spirit of transparency, I will share lessons, revelations, and nuggets that life has gifted to me throughout my process. There are certainly gifts I would love to return to sender at times, but I must keep them and learn. It is my hope and prayer that something written between these pages will resonate with you, assist you, and prick your spirit as you experience your own transformation and ascension. Remember, perfection is not the destination, but becoming better with each passing moment.

Ready? Let's go! Grab my wings as we take flight and soar!

"You haven't seen the best of me,
I'm still working on my masterpiece."
~Jessie

The Breakdown

*"Maybe the prize is the ability to endure;
in knowing that you had the fire inside of you
to survive the process."*
~LB

I get so excited each time I read the introduction! While authoring this book It moves me when I think about the Phoenix that lies within you. The Phoenix of the legends is fictitious, but you are not. You are a real, breathing, flesh and blood embodiment of all that is powerful about this amazing bird. You are ripe and ready to rise! You are no longer content with rolling in the ashes. YOU can do it! I can do it. WE can do it!

Before we dive into the steak and potatoes of this work (tofu for my non-meat eaters), I want to share the breakdown of each chapter. Each section has the following segments:

- **What** is the concept/lesson?
- **Why** is it important to ascension?
- **How** can it be done?
- **Transformational Transparency** (My Personal Experience)
- **Fuel for Flight**

I employed this method to provide you with a smooth journey through this written work. It was penned with you in mind. You deserve to meet the absolute best version of yourself, the pentacle of everything you were created to be and do on this Earth. My deepest desire is that you never be satisfied with mediocrity, and that you feel so unsettled in anything

> "My deepest desire is that you never be satisfied with mediocrity..."

other than greatness that you feel compelled to move on your own behalf. To this end, I have put the most expensive lessons and concepts I have learned between these pages. My ascension has been tumultuous and beautiful, an incomplete work of art. I am confident that yours will be as well.

Although parts of this book may warm your soul and make you laugh, others may not. Certain words may cause discomfort, others may be soothingly familiar. Either way, I pray that you remember that I have nothing but the purest intentions for you as I share my life education. Our journey through this realm is a huge university, with our experiences as the coursework. We strive to earn straight A's, but in our humanness, we sometimes miss the mark. That's okay, because the spirit of excellence within you gives the nudge to do better with each go around.

Change is not always easy nor glamorous, except when changing clothes or classes, and even these events can get a little hairy. Ascension requires the most pivotal change of all, the changing of your mind. Therefore, it is messy. You are going to have to go to war with yourself to make it happen, committing to battle after battle. You will be knocked down and your will must pull you back up. There may be someday days when, like I did just the other day, you cry out "I'm tired! Can't I just be average?!"

Let me answer that for you. NO! You may NOT be average. You may NOT settle. You may NOT give up. You may NOT relegate yourself to a life of "less than." You may NOT allow your mind to make independent, executive decisions regarding the actions that you will take. You WILL be extraordinary! You WILL require more, do more, and be more! You WILL build a legacy! You WILL force your mind to bend to your will! You WILL endure! You WILL fight for it all! In the end, it WILL be worth it!

YOU WILL RISE LIKE THE PHOENIX YOU ARE AND THE WORLD WILL REMEMBER YOUR NAME!

"God help you if you are a Phoenix and

dare to rise up from the ash."

~Alana Davis

Slay

Your

Dragons

Dragon:

a mythical reptilian-like creature that in European tradition symbolized chaos, evil, or disorder.

W*hat?*

Warning: The preliminary phase of your ascension ride will be a little turbulent, maybe even chaotic. Not to worry, the great philosopher Ralph Waldo Emerson said, "All great change is preceded by chaos." To get traction, we must begin by slaying dragons. You might be saying, "What?" to yourself right now. Slaying dragons? For some, the word "dragon" conjures up images of fire-breathing monsters and Sir Lancelot's sword Excalibur. Well, I can assure you that the kinds of dragons that I am talking about here do breathe fire and are monstrous. But with Excalibur's sword and your own determination, you will subjugate them!

Have you ever battled anxiety or depression? Do you have secret inner conversations with others in which you silently say, "Like me, approve of me, make me matter?" Low-self-esteem, poor self-image, or paralyzing lack of self-confidence peeking through your window? Dysfunction? Trauma? Rejection or abandonment issues? Ah, I know, you struggle with what the legendary Dr. Martin Luther King coined "your own sense of 'somebodiness'?" Well, let me drop a nugget in the bucket for you. *These* are *dragons*. If you've seen a dragon on tv, or in the movies, you know that they are gigantic, scary, and dangerous. They paralyze their victims with fear. This is the power and nature of dragons.

Dragons are any beliefs you have about yourself, the world, and your place in it that impede your capacity to live a healthy, fulfilled life. They are strongholds that, until the grip is broken, suspend you in a state of captivity. Some people call them demons or giants. Whichever label one chooses to describe them, if they do not serve you well, changes may be in order. I know that the term "slaying" might sound slightly over the top, but those stubborn intrusive thoughts, behaviors, and baggage may require it. Though "slaying" may bring to mind thoughts of violence and mayhem, this is far from the intent of this book. Here, "slaying" simply means bringing negativity under submission, and releasing positivity and peace in its place.

As troublesome as these creatures and minions are, they can be subdued with the proper strategies and tools. You can't just go after a dragon willy nilly and think you will escape unscathed. There is a method to accomplishing this Herculean impossible feat. It will take a well-devised plan and precise execution, which we will discuss later in the chapter. The sturdiest, most durable tool you will need going into the battle is your "why." Without your "why," the mission may be jeopardized before it begins.

W*hy?*

This tiny word is one of the most powerful in the English language. It has multiple meanings, but for the purposes of our discussion it refers to two simple words: your reason. Before you decide to take on these dragons that have sown chaos and confusion into your life, you had better figure out why you are doing it. I can tell you unequivocally that if you are not crystal clear concerning your reasons for engaging these monsters on the battlefield, you will be going home on your shield, not carrying it. In the thickest part of my battle, I took my eyes off my "why," and ended up pointed in the wrong direction on a two-lane highway. Please don't do that.

Simply put, your "why" must be strong enough, and clear enough, to carry you through your darkest moments. As you walk through the valley of dry bones that are your hindering "isms," there will be moments when the pain and frustration will not seem to be worth it. You are not going to feel like a warrior in all seasons. There will be moments when retreating and surrendering won't seem like bad options. This is where your "why" comes into play.

Your "why" drags you out of bed in the morning when depression wants to keep you sedated. Your "why" will cause you to destroy any thoughts that interfere with your goals and objectives. It snaps you back into focus when your thoughts run amuck. Your reason for slaying your dragons is the carrot life dangles in front of your face to get you to move! It makes you reach

> "Your "why" will cause you to destroy any thoughts that interfere with your goals and objectives."

and stretch until you grab hold of the reward received in return for your efforts. It incites a yearning to RISE!

I would be a billionaire if I had a shiny coin for each time my "why" pulled me through. My three babies are the reason that I refuse to let the dragon win the fight for my life. Just between you and I, there were a couple of tight moments when I wondered if even those reasons would be enough. Dragons can be ruthless and unyielding. Strongholds take root deep down inside of a person. Dragons and the little minions they produce are formidable opponents. Formidable, but not invincible, if your "why" is clear. What's your why?

How?

We have acknowledged the power of the dragon. Well, YOU have the same power! In this section you learn how to use that power through strategies and tools to subdue your dragons.

We have been introduced to the foundational bricks we can use to subdue him. Yes, I pluralized "battles" and "dragons." It is rare that a person only has a singular issue to overcome. Therefore, there must be multiple battles. If you have ever watched a war movie, you will observe that seldom does a single battle win a war. War typically involves engagements over time, the conclusion of which is the result of one side's retreat, surrender, or annihilation. In our case, retreat nor surrender are on the table. Victory is the ONLY option.

Because my dragons were especially stubborn, I followed specific steps to bring them under submission:

- ✓ **Identify**
- ✓ **Study**
- ✓ **Devise and Execute**

Before I go on, I will own the fact that this section has an air of warmongering to it. This is for good reason. Fighting against yourself, to free yourself, *is* a war of epic proportions. I want to clarify that the dragons I am addressing in this section are not external. They are the ones that lie within us. Little of the ascension process is about anyone outside of us. The primary battles are always primarily within.

I*dentify*

The rationale behind this step is simple: I couldn't win a fight against an unknown enemy. How would I know who or what the target is?

Imagine this: you receive an anonymous call from a man with a raspy voice directing you to go to a gala event and take out the enemy. He reveals the location the of the weapon, as well as the escape plans. He discloses key details about the party such as the address, appropriate attire, and commencement time. After providing more ancillary details, the mysterious gentleman abruptly terminates the call. Notice any missing pieces of critical information? Go ahead, re-read this scenario, then take a few seconds to think about it.

I'm sure the Sherlock in you hit the nail right on the head. Our puppet master neglected to leave out a particularly important piece of information. He gave no particulars about the target whatsoever. Is the enemy a male or female? What does he/she look like? What will the person be wearing? What is the individual's role/function at the party? The answers to these questions would be extremely helpful. Not only would more information assist in engaging the correct target, but it would significantly decrease the margin of error. Moreover, clear identification of the enemy affords one the opportunity to study him.

This is exactly what we will face if we don't identify our dragons. If we have no clue what we are fighting, how do we know how to fight? My rising taught me to ask myself poignant questions in this area. What character traits, habits, or mindsets have been detrimental to my growth? What are areas in which I would like to improve? Are there particular biases or limiting beliefs that have held me back? Armed with this information, I could confidently advance to the next step.

Study

The great Chinese general Sun Tzu wrote in the timeless war strategy guide *The Art of War*, "Know the enemy and know yourself and you need not fear the result of a hundred battles." I cannot emphasize this enough, fellow risers. You must study the dragons before you fight them! Please do not attempt to battle what you have not researched. You will be walking into a gun fight with a yoyo expecting to do real damage. The only injuries sustained entering the scene under those circumstances will be a slight knot on the eye and possible middle finger fatigue.

So, what should we be looking for? Patterns. Triggers. History. For example, when is your anxiety usually triggered? Is there a particular person, place, or situation that seems to bring about attacks? Are there certain words or phrases that take your mind back to a dark place? Once you have pondered the answers to these questions, switch angles: What are your typical responses to these dragons? How do you behave when depressed, anxious, or afraid? Do you self-medicate? If so, in what ways? Is there a tendency to go inward and hide, or go outward and pull others into your struggle? Reflecting on these types of questions is a terrific way to engage in self-exploration. Doing so gives us the intel we need to progress smoothly into the next step.

D*evise* and E*xecute*

Now we're getting down to the good part. Liberation is steps away, but those steps are going to be long and cumbersome. No worries, though. Your "why" will get you there! The tough moments and preparation through study have given you the tactical advantage. You thought deeply about the discovery questions mentioned earlier, which gave you crucial information about yourself and the enemy. Remember that General Tzu told us that if we know ourselves and the enemy, we will be alright. You will be more than prepared! Remember, execution is the key to victory!

At this point, I will let you in on the strategies that have worked for me thus far:

א **Intentional Engagement:** I make every effort to engage energy that is positive and life-giving. I make room for things that make me feel safe, warm, and joyous. When negativity sneaks into my mind space and tries to turn my smile into a frown, I practice energy shifting. I summon the morning sun to appear with its healing rays. It honors my request every time and adjusts the atmosphere.

א **Tool Belt:** In case the dragon wants to breathe fire my way, I have something on tap ready to go. I quickly whip out a song, affirmation, Bible verse, or quote that diametrically opposes the thought. Immediately the power of light overtakes the darkness, and my spirit is returned to its blissful state. These intrusive thoughts are no match for my Wonder Woman Positive Thought Bracelets!

א **Self-Care:** I will disclose right now that you might get sick of seeing these two words throughout this book. Words cannot express the value of loving yourself and taking care of your mental, spiritual, and physical needs. Self-care builds your inner core and creates a person so strong that the dragons' fire can cause no harm. It will be that weapon that is formed but doesn't prosper.

א **Therapy/Counseling:** Therapy gets to root of the issues and slowly begins to diminish the dragon's power position. It calls out the dragons by name, one by one, so that they can be dealt with appropriately. This is how you become strong and steady enough to stand your ground.

Transformational Transparency

Trauma and bullying gave rise to anxiety, which then, created an identity crisis. The identity crisis caused me to forget who I was (a child of the Most High, beautiful, intelligent, kind, worthy), thereby producing less-than-stellar behavior patterns as I progressed into adulthood.

Let us go a little deeper. The effects of trauma became a prison that I, at the time, did not possess the tools to break free from. It generated a "hamster wheel effect." Traumatic event takes place, I attempt to deal with it on my own, attempt fails, I move through life as if nothing happened, stage is set for repeat...a cycle more vicious than a ticked off shrew! It was every bit like the movie Ground Hog's Day (if you haven't seen it, you should check it out).

This not-so-floral smelling potpourri of circumstances and after-effects birthed a hydra that rivals that of any sci-fi movie. What makes it more interesting is that my hydra's head had names: anxiety, self-deprecation, distorted self-image, rejection, abandonment, loneliness, attachment issues, poor judge of character, recklessness. That is nine, isn't it? There may be more, but a hydra only has nine heads, so we will stick to these for now. The point is that this hydra was fierce like a model on a Paris runway! Yes, honey, one hydra procreated and made a bunch of little baby hydras that caused all types of mischief in my life.

So, here is where I messed up big time, and where I am pleading with you not to do the same. Through the grace of the Creator, I made it out of my "basement" moments alive, but I was surviving, but not thriving. Yes, I was still breathing, smiling, going to school, raising a family, and going through the motions of life, but I was not living my best life. Why? The reasons are two-fold and interconnected: 1) I did not tell anyone about what occurred who could appropriately and effectively deal with the situation, and 2) I did not seek professional help. Please hear me, silence is not okay when it comes to getting the help you need after experiencing ANY type of trauma. Silence can be a form of avoidance, and avoidance is a one-way ticket to Breakdownsville. I have been there, and I would not recommend it as a vacation spot.

You might be taken aback at the candor with which I've shared these spotty details of my past. Rest assured, I am okay with it. I know, without a shadow of a doubt, that transparency is necessary for healing. I believe that one person's courage to testify gives others permission to do the same. As my grandmother always said, better out than in. Remember, the dragon's roar gets louder the more silent we are. Speak your truth. Be bold, unafraid, and unashamed!

It Takes a Village

There is an extremely important piece to this puzzle that it would be an abomination to omit. I did not, nor could I, do this alone! I repeat, this was not a solo effort! In fact, I was not even aware that I was in breakdown, though I was right in the thick of it. It took a tribe of warriors, a colony of angels to work in concert to bring me through. They graciously helped me gather what was left of my righteous mind. It was the collective effort of individuals who loved me enough to sacrifice time, finances, and energy to assist me in my dragon-slaying efforts. Stay with me, this part is important, and I need you to get this.

Those rising Phoenixes reading this book raised in urban areas may be familiar with the infamous "windmill." The "windmill' is a defensive combat tactic utilized particularly by females. It involves turning the head to either side, closing both eyes, and flailing the arms wildly into the air the way a windmill rotates. It is quite a sight to see, I assure you. The problem with this tactic is that you can't hit anything if your eyes are closed. I mean, isn't the whole point to make contact? Otherwise, you just have two people out there looking like human fans trying to cool off an entire crowd. Pointless.

In your case, you will not have to worry about this colossal waste of energy because you have villagers to help you out. You may not believe it, but you do. Even if you must play R & B singer Rihanna's line "SOS, please somebody help me..." at full volume, do whatever you need to do to get somebody by your side. You will be shocked at who will show up. One of the dragon's best plays is getting you to believe that you are alone in the fight. Don't buy it, not even for a dollar.

It took quite some time for me to fully believe that I am strong, resilient, and fully capable of subduing my dragons. I just needed to begin the process by turning and facing them. As you read this, maybe there are some things, some minions that you need to process through also. Well, I say we applaud ourselves as we submit to the freedom and purpose process. I am so excited for us! We have a village cheering us on from the sidelines. Can you hear them? This is our moment. Health and liberty are ours for the taking if we do the work. Step 1 down, six more to go. We've got this!

F*uel* for F*light*

Slaying your dragons is difficult, but worth every moment of the struggle. This is how you begin to build your internal command center. The incredible part is that

"You owe it to yourself and your "why" to take those dragons to task."

you have everything you need inside of you to make it happen. Executing the strategies that you have learned here and those that you acquire on your own will ensure your success and freedom. You owe it to yourself and your "why" to take those dragons to task. Although the battle is inherently yours to fight alone, don't be ashamed to shout and summon your tribe for help. Even if you don't think you have a tribe, shout anyway. You will be amazed at what can happen with a quick shout out for help.

Knowledge:

*the state of being aware of something
or having information*

W*hat?*

Whew! Are you okay after that last chapter? I know, things got a chaotic back there, but as the world-famous philosopher Ralph Waldo Emerson stated, "all great change is preceded by chaos." Your transformation will be one of the greatest occurrences the world has ever known! To that end, it was crucial to slay those dragons and get a good running start to your next destination: self-discovery. When you slay your dragons, freedom rings and reigns. Your mind, spirit, and soul now have space to breathe and move around. Bondages are broken and shackles are released. Tattered and torn from battle, you can now walk out into the light and receive the blessings of your victory. Stronger and wiser, you can smile and savor the moment, knowing that up is the only way to go from here! Now, you are ready for the next step in your transformation.

> "Imagine opening your front door and being greeting by a lighter, more joyous version of yourself."

As you walk boldly into your destiny, you get to engage in my favorite activity, self-discovery. This is such a marvelous place to be because it presents a myriad of possibilities. You're not where you were, but you're not quite where you are headed. That's what makes it so wonderful! You have the privilege of meeting yourself all over again in your brand-new state of awesomeness! Doesn't that sound refreshing? You are free dahling. Imagine opening your front door and being greeting by a lighter, more joyous version of yourself. Visualize having tea while conversing with the new you. Can you see that beautiful, infectious smile? Does the thought of warm energy send electricity through your body? This is the by-product of your renewed sense of confidence and esteem.

Attraction, Alignment, and Actualization

My journey of self-discovery revealed three key elements: Attraction, Alignment, and Actualization. In my estimation, these elements provide the framework for ascension in its most authentic form. Once the discovery work is done, the energy most suited to your purpose shows up. Synergy forms, and combined you become unstoppable!

Attraction

The law of attraction explains nicely how and why this element is so pivotal. Simply put, we attract whatever we are, as well as whatever we *believe* ourselves to be. As an extension, our actions fall right in line and reflect these beliefs. The world at large takes note, consciously or unconsciously, of our actions. Those of like minds are drawn to us. Before we know it, everything is moving in the same direction.

There is another piece to the attraction concept. In addition to attracting energy spirits, you repel what is incongruent with your essence. You will notice that as you progress toward proper positioning and actualization, those not slated to be a member of your herd will begin to slowly fall off. The frequency and duration of interactions gradually diminishes, until, in cases, it will cease altogether. This is not necessarily a terrible thing and is not meant to demote nor reduce the value of anyone. Depending upon who it is, it may hurt, and that's okay. Some people are meant to bless our lives for a reason and a season.

Alignment

As previously mentioned, alignment is the desired fruit of attraction. When the right people and situations enter your life, you begin to move in alignment toward your ascension. Alignment simply means that all the people and circumstances in your life begin to travel in the same direction as your purpose and destiny, working for you and not against you. Attraction is a critical component of alignment because alignment cannot occur if you attract and keep the wrong energy into your life. It's like trying to drive a car whose steering wheel only turns left; you will never get anywhere. Believe me, I continue to learn and grow in this area with each passing day. Growth is uncomfortable and difficult at times, but in my estimation, well worth it!

> "Alignment simply means that all the people and circumstances in your life begin to travel in the same direction as your purpose and destiny,..."

Actualization

Actualization is the grand and glorious by-product of attraction and alignment. This is where you receive the gift of authenticity of self. It's when you get to live life in full and out loud! Did that last statement put a smile on your face? Actualization brings forth an awakening, a realization of who you are as a person. You get to witness the manifestation of the you that was always meant to be. This allows you to see yourself accurately and flow accordingly. Purpose is revealed and recognized. Every morning becomes an opportunity!

W*hy?*

One of the biggest lessons I have learned to date is this: If you do not know who you are, other people will tell you who you are. If you are lucky, it will be someone who has the best of intentions towards you. If you pull the short straw, your identity will be compromised and assigned by someone who cares nothing about you or your well-being. It's like a craps game in Vegas. I say, why risk crapping out? Why not take the fabulous journey toward learning who you are for yourself? That way, you steer the boat and show others the identity you have chosen for yourself. Once you have established your identity no one can take it away from you unless you surrender it.

I found the process of self-discovery to be delectable! A solid, strong self-identity oozes self confidence and self-esteem. I realize that it is my responsibility to teach others how to treat me, establishing clear boundaries and expectations. I am figuring out what I want and don't want, what I like and don't like, and what I will and will not accept. My steps are becoming ordered and aligned. There is a clearer picture of my place in the Earth. Peace is establishing itself, and ascension is inevitable.

H*ow?* (Isolation, Quality Time w/Self, Self-Care)

This journey has been tough, to say the least. Is it fine for me to use the words weird, or strange, to describe it? Either way, it has also been bountifully rewarding. I have a workout t-shirt that says, "No pain, no champagne." That means that if I want the celebration, I must go through the process (I don't know how I feel about that dirty little word). The self-discovery piece of this process has been irrefutably essential. I am paying attention to myself more, noticing things that I applaud, as well as things that I need to improve upon. I was totally unaware that I had just let myself go to pot!7 All in all, I feel like a better mother, friend, sister, daughter, and overall person. Focusing on myself just feels good.

I*solation*

In the past when I herd the word isolation, visions of being stranded on an island alone, spending my days talking to a soccer ball named Wilson, came to mind. Yup, I could just see myself fighting hermit crabs for the last morsel of food, like Tom Hanks' character in the movie Castaway. Doesn't sound like fun, does it? Then the COVID lockdown of 2020 provided me with an entirely new and different frame of reference for the word isolation. I showed me that being alone is not necessarily synonymous with being lonely. I experienced the peace, self-connection, and rejuvenation that can come with quiet time away. The lockdown time period, in particular, was a tremendous blessing for myself, my family, and for millions of people who just needed to breathe.

Now, I make time for periodic intentional isolation. I cannot imagine EVER allowing myself to get to that point of burnout again where I place myself in physical, mental, spiritual, and emotional jeopardy. I am thankful for the blessing of refocus, refining, and rejuvenation. I'm sure my children are happy that I found my mind, also. What I do understand is that taking time for oneself must be deliberate and planned. Here are some ways that I implemented isolation in my own life during my pre-ascension phase:

How I isolated:

- ℵ **Establish boundaries:** I guarded my time and space. An invisible perimeter was set up around my mind, heart, and spirit. It was unusual and I felt guilty initially, which eventually dissipated. This did wonders for my mental and spiritual well-being.
- ℵ **Set a media schedule:** I instituted a schedule for phone, computer, and TV use. Social media usage was slowed to a crawl. The computer became a workstation. Telephone conversations were cut in half.
- ℵ **Limit human interaction (when possible):** Aside from those within my household, the only people I interacted with regularly were the folks at the grocery store, gas station, and fitness center.

QT with Self

While eating the fruit from the beautiful trees on self-imposed isolation island, I got to spend quality time with myself. I accepted that it was okay to steal away and enjoy my own company. It was okay, and *necessary*. This is how I began to fall in love with myself. These small adjustments unearthed my self-worth and fortified my self-image. The waves that washed upon the shore revealed the subtle nuances of my uniqueness.

Ways to find out who you are:

- ℵ **Poignant Questioning:** I asked myself the following types of exploratory questions: What makes me smile? What causes fear? What gives goosebumps and tingles? What fabric do I like to feel against my skin? Whose company brings me the most joy? Finding the answers to questions like these was an eye-opening experience that taught me new things about myself.

- **Thought Monitoring:** Journaling is a fantastic way to do this. Periodically record your thoughts on paper or electronically, especially first thing in the morning and right before falling asleep. These are key times when your subconscious mind is free and unhindered.
- **Self-Dating:** I know this may sound odd, but it has been so rewarding! One night a week I take myself on a date. The location could be somewhere outside of the house, like a movie or restaurant. Most of the time I prefer to keep it indoors, preparing myself a delicious meal or reading an enjoyable book. Treating myself to a mani/pedi is always fun as well.

Self-Care (My personal favorite)

How do I practice self-care? Let me count the ways. Self-care has become my favorite step in self-discovery. I find it to be a logical follow-up to steps 1 and 2. After spending time alone uncovering who you are through questioning and observation, I took that information and performed corresponding acts of self-love and self-healing. It is the perfect wrap up to the ultimate trip. Let me tell you, whether male or female, this part is hot!

Methods of self-care:

- **Graceful Declining:** I learned to take care of myself by saying "No" when necessary and not succumbing to guilt when I did. It took me time to understand that declining gracefully was my right, as well as a key component of self-care.
- **Spa Days:** Yes, yes, and yes! Massages, manicures, pedicures, facials...all of it! These are nutrients for the mind, body, and spirit. They make us feel and look good. When we are looking and feeling magnificent, we glow! When I'm budgeting, I just head down to the

local dollar store and purchase items for an at-home spa day. It is equally as enjoyable!

ℵ **Nature walks:** Nature is the Creator's gift to us all and has incredible healing properties. A walk through the forest preserves or brisk stroll outside in the neighborhood increases blood flow and releases "feel good" chemicals in your brain. Sitting on a beach has a similar effect. The body experiences an actual "high" from being in nature.

ℵ **Physical Self-Care:** Our body is your temple, and we need it to carry us through each day with maximum effectiveness. Improper function limits the richness of our existence. In my case, I needed to seriously level up in this area. Regular checkups were placed into regular rotation, and I hightailed it to the doctor when symptoms of illness appeared. This was a huge adjustment for me!

ℵ **Mental/Emotional Self-Care:** The above also applies to our mental health. If the mind is not functioning correctly, NOTHING flows properly. The mind is our wheelhouse and will kick in when the body gives out. The brain/body connection orchestrates every move we make. The condition/state of our mind is linked to perceptions, thoughts, and actions. In fact, the mind can make a healthy body sick. I learned to feed my mind a diet of positivity and uplifting thoughts. I began seeing a therapist, resting my mind frequently. Allowing love and light to permeate me made an incredible difference!

Transformational Transparency

I can recall as clearly as day the Wednesday morning during the COVID-19 forced rest period (that's what I call the lockdown) when I looked at my toes for the first time in years. I had seen them, of course, but had not *looked* at them. I wiggled them and stared in fascination at the hot pink color on them. When I rolled over to grab my phone, my left hand brushed up against my right arm. The ensuing foreign sensation was a reminder that I hadn't touch my own skin in eons. It was beautiful, bizarre, and strange simultaneously. Can you believe that when I walked past the mirror, I had forgotten what I looked like? My self-neglect was in full effect! That moment marked the commencement of my self-rediscovery phase.

Self-discovery has been an incredible experience. Taking time to revisit what makes my senses go wild has been unparalleled. There is a peace in my soul now that surpasses even my own understanding. Awareness and intuition levels are at an all-time high. I trust myself more. I have learned to, as my grandfather says, try a spirit by a spirit. That

> "I trust myself more."

means I engage based upon how a person makes me feel in their presence. My self-concept is coming together nicely, which is feeding my self-esteem a healthy diet of confidence. Faith has taken the wheel as my self-belief has skyrocketed. Self-date nights are amazing!

Heightened self-cognizance has made another astounding difference. The harmony and serenity have settled in my heart, sparking a reconciliation with my core. It is as if I am floating above anything negative or petty. Love has penetrated and insulated me against disempowering thoughts and harmful energy. Spending time exploring what makes me tick made me fall in love with myself. This love led me to reach an unexpected level of forgiveness, both of myself and others. I'm telling you, self-awareness is every- thing!

F*uel* for F*light*

I believe that to know oneself is to love oneself. The self-discovery process is nothing short of miraculous! Becoming gentler and more compassionate with myself has enabled me to be better for those who I care about. I can feel your excitement as you brainstorm ways to love yourself in new and amazing ways. There is a comfort and strength in knowing unequivocally who you are and where you fit in the jigsaw puzzle of life. Self-love is neither selfish nor weak. It is one of the unselfish things any person can do. Enjoy getting to know you. You are a person well worth knowing!

Default

Status

Adjustment

Default:

What exists or happens unless someone changes it.

Default (2):

To make a selection automatically in the absence of a choice made by the user.

W*hat?*

Now that we have overthrown those dragons and recaptured our identity, we have wiggle room to make remarkable things happen. The next step to takeoff involves changing the default status in the brain. The brain is one big supercomputer that controls everything that happens in association with the body. Also like a computer, it is a processing center that interprets and catalogues inputs and outputs. Imagine a large external hard drive filled to the max with movies, pictures, applications, and other types of files. Whatever is downloaded is what exists there. Those baby dragons were viruses that snuck inside the hard drive, causing a system malfunction.

What exactly is one's default status? It is comprised of the habitual thoughts and actions that your brain returns to any time you experience life's events. "Every time something like this happens, I think like this." "Whenever someone says that about me, I respond that way." For instance, prior to my default status adjustment, my default was anxiety. It was as if someone was always standing over me with that darn shoe ready to drop it at any given moment. My brain stayed ready, so it didn't have to get ready. Just like the caveman days. You know, when there was always something ferocious lurking around every corner. When a person remains in this mode over a prolonged period, anxiety is the result.

W*hy?*

Motivational speaker, author, and entrepreneur, Bertina Power, said it best, "Either you can be pitiful or POWERful, but you can't be both. So, I say be POWERful!" I love this quote because it encompasses the reason default status is so important, especially in the rising process. Life's foolery and challenges can inherently make one feel pitiful, weak, and incapable. That reaction is natural and okay...at first. Then you must ask the question, "Are you pitiful or powerful?" Phoenixes choose the latter. This is where ascension be- gins, in the mindset shift. The moment you decide that no longer rolling around in the ashes is the ONLY option, the universe will meet you in that place.

> "Are you pitiful or powerful?" Phoenixes choose the latter.

The decision to change your default status is personal. You, and only you, can choose to do what is necessary to soar. I believe in self-questioning and self-reflection to arrive at pivotal answers concerning our lives. One question must revolve around the willingness and necessity to transition your mindset. In my own transformative experience, default status modifications were not an option. They were generating behavior patterns that simply were not working. I became self-destructive, allowing myself and others to treat me any old kind of way. They were blocking my blessings, preventing me from walking in my purpose. I had, and still have, serious work to do on this Earth, and that anxiety-driven default status was doing nothing to forge me ahead.

Do you want to be successful? Are there hopes, dreams, and aspirations that you have for your life? Is legacy-building on your list of objectives? If you are reading this book, my guess is that the answer to those questions is "yes." My response to all three questions is a booming "YES!" Everything that I do at this point centers around these three points. The proper mindset and default status is the only way I will successful. Mindset and default drives perspective, and as motivational speaker Inky Johnson so eloquently put it, perspective drives performance. Goal-reaching is performance and action-driven, actions that originate from our mindset. Whatever is needed to bring our default status into alignment with those goals is the appropriate course of action. This is a major reason our default status must shift if necessary.

H*ow?*

Mindset shifting is not for the weak or faint of heart. You must be smart enough to outwit your own psyche. Have you ever tried prying a school-aged child out of bed on a Monday morning after a two-day weekend? Your mindset puts up the same kind of resistance to change. It lies in a warm bed under blankets of familiarity, viewing notable change with upset. That is okay because you are a Master Mind Manipulator. With intentional and consistent effort, you can bring your mind around to producing the kinds of thought that bear positive results. I achieved results in my own life through a 3-pronged method I continue to use to aide in my healing process (**Decide, Disrupt, Do**):

D*ecide* (Examine, Analyze, Decide)

Any type of adjustment begins with a firm, definitive decision. The decision flips the switch and tells your mind that business as usual has ceased. The decision must be solid. There can be no wavering once you start the process. If things do get a little shaky, quickly bring your mind back into position. You can do this by looking at a picture of your "why," revisiting your vision board, or listening to something motivational. In the beginning, your mind will resist! You are stronger than the resistance. You are a Phoenix. Use your powers to subjugate your thoughts. Let your "why" solidify your decision.

- **Examine:** The ground floor place where I started was examining patterns and outcomes. It wasn't until I stopped and paid attention that I noticed there were repeated patterns of behavior stemming from trauma. Upon further investigation, I realized that these patterns had been preventing me from living my best life, which, in turn, effected my children and my family. Eventually I asked myself some tough questions: 1) Which behaviors were detracting from my life, 2) Where did these ideas and behaviors originate? When I began getting that part figured out, there was one last question I asked myself: Was my growth being hindered? My answer was yes, so I went to Step 2. If yours is the same, the next section may be helpful.

- **Analyze:** If the answer to any of the above is yes, then it is time to do cost-benefit analysis. What is allowing this detracting energy costing you? Time, health, productivity? The benefit portion is the other piece. Is what you receive from maintaining that energy or habit worth it? Is it serving you, your family, or your purpose well? In other words, is the price for continued engagement with these self-defeating actions and thoughts worth the benefits? If not, move to step 3.

- **Decide:** This part is often the most difficult. After examining and doing cost/benefit analysis, you have to then decide unequivocally that you will do what it takes to make the appropriate and required changes.

D *isrupt* (Interrupt, Erase, Replace)

Once you decide, it is time to disrupt the patterns and stop those destiny-stealing thoughts right in their tracks. The first law of physics says that objects in motion stay in motion until met with a force strong enough to stop it. In my case, outside assistance was necessary for the disruption. Villagers lovingly and silently helped me move those debilitating thought patterns toward extinction through interruption and modeling. I had to be open and humble enough to accept the help.

- ℵ **Interrupt:** This is an example of how I have used interruption in my own journey: One of my defaults is what I term "anxiety calling." It was like "phone-a-friend" whenever I felt too disconnected from the world. Stems from childhood stuff, you know? To assist me in this moving this pattern toward extinction, I asked loved ones to not take my calls at times, as difficult as it may be. This interrupts the continuity of the pattern, leading my brain to slowly, but surely, disconnect and disassociate that activity as a default. This transitions you to the next phase.

- ℵ **Erase:** Sooner or later, when a certain thought or behavior is consistently interrupted, it is erased. Sometimes not entirely, but certainly significantly. Continue to interrupt those unwanted patterns. Deprive them of oxygen so you can breathe freely! Now you are on to the next step.

- ℵ **Replace:** The Law of Conservation of Mass states, in short, that when there is a physical or chemical change, the amount of matter remains the same, just the form changes. This is how I can best illustrate the replacement portion of this overarching step. When we erase undesired thoughts and actions, there is still that cognitive space there. It's like when you pull something off the shelf at Walgreens, leaving an empty space where the product used to be. That night, an employee does what is called "facing," meaning, the product is replaced to fill the gap. This is what must happen when we erase the old; something new has to take its place. This is how new habits are formed. Interruption tells the brain what we *do not* want. It needs specific instructions on how it is to behave *now*. Otherwise, it will default back to the same old, same old, and we do NOT want that! The brain needs a new menu to select from. I have included an illustration in the next paragraph.

What does this look like? Imagine being a fly on the wall when celebrity chef Gerry Garvin (if you haven't heard of him, you should look him up) is revamping someone's struggling restaurant. Maybe a number of menu items are outdated, or they just are not well-prepared. In either instance, the great and powerful chef determines that removal is necessary to save the restaurant. Various dishes remain, others are set free. What happens then? Gerry may choose to replace them with fresh, new menu options that taste better and have much more customer appeal. In the end, current customers have a renewed interest in the establishment, and new customers eagerly anticipate getting a taste of the delectable new meal options!

Sounds promising, doesn't it? This is exactly what happens when we have the courage to decide and disrupt! We break the chains of harmful behavior. No matter the environment, exposure, or experiences, those circumstances do not get to dictate the trajectory of the rest of our existence. A changed mind leads to changed actions. Changed actions alter habits. Altered habits transform your life. We can keep what works and get rid of what does not. Our lives life, our rules. This is how we RISE!

D*o* (Resist, Block, Execute)

- ℵ **Resist:** "Resist the devil and he will flee" (James 4:7, KJV). I am not advocating for any specific religion in the book; however, I do find that this verse demonstrates my point well. Once you become aware of what needs to change, and decide to submit to the process, temptation always lurks around the corner. ALWAYS. Your brain, like me with my favorite songs, likes to replay the same thing repeatedly. Those songs are familiar, *and* I know all the words. I'm asking that you join me in defying the temptation to revisit those old playing fields (not the songs, I'm going to keep doing that). I mean the urge to return to those things we worked so hard to eradicate. I struggle often with this one, and that is fine. Struggle proves that we are trying. Grace will accompany our progress.

- ℵ **Block:** When those defiant thoughts do come, and they will, a plan to block them will take care of that! I use my mental Wakanda warrior bracelets to do the job for me. When an unnerving thought enters my serenity space, I hold up each wrist and say "unbothered" with each invisible band, and the thoughts dissipate. Sometimes it takes a few zaps, but eventually, the mission is successful.

- ℵ **Execute:** This is where a new life begins take form. Each time a thought or action is replaced or interrupted; new connections are formed. The more this happens, the stronger the connections become. As I implemented this step with gradually increasing consistency, I noticed a change in my outlook and perspective.

Here is where I messed up initially and continue to struggle periodically. After disrupting the patterns, it helps to do all you can to resist the urge to go back and sip the Kool-Aid. If it didn't taste good before, it is likely that much has changed. If it has, and it now tastes amazing AND quenches your thirst, keep drinking! If not, pour it down the sink and grab water. How do I know? I went back...multiple times. I hold the line, then get lax and lose my grip. What do I do? Give myself a good "talking to" (the tone of which varies depending on the day) and pick that line right back up. Habits are tremendously difficult to break. It was necessary for me to set up systems to block those thoughts when they wanted to return to that old default. I was NOT about to go back to hell. The only fire I wanted to be consumed by was the one that lit up my wings.

An example of a system that I put in place for "anxiety calling" is each time I felt the urge to pick up the phone, I studied a foreign language instead (one of my favorite activities). The goal is to have something to do in place of the behavior you are seeking to disrupt. Another activity I did in place of the call is working out or reading. Remember when we talked about our toolbelt strategies? This is an excellent example of what that looks like. You want to already have a positive alternate behavior ready to go to replace the undesired one. Isn't that impressive? It's a win-win!

After careful reflection, you will come to know the right course of action for you. Remember to do something you love and enjoy, but that is healthy and helpful as your replacement activity. This is where the magnificent work of default status replacement is done. Also, trust your instincts and listen to your internal voice. They will lead you along the correct path concerning best practices for your growth and healing.

Transformational Transparency

Of the myriad of lessons that I have learned in preparation for my ascension, those surrounding the power of the human mind were the most important. I have come to respect and revere the mind and brain's capacity to create whatever reality we desire. It was not until I gained a reasonable command over my default status and perception that I made true progress. For years I lived as a helpless victim of my story. Now, I seize the reigns of control over my thoughts. This is what the Phoenix transformation is all about!

In the spirit of transparency, I will share that I am authoring this book while pushing through a memory loss issue. The residual effects of constant stress and trauma over an extended period caused a system overload, and my brain simply said, "Since you won't stop, I'm going to stop for you!" As my fingers are typing I am praying that these words make sense, since my brain is digging through files trying to find my pre-ascension vocabulary. For those who were unaware, trauma and stress have a direct impact on memory and brain function. I am being candid with this information because I want anyone struggling to know that he or she is not alone.

Now, back to perception and default status. My healing was kicked into warp speed the moment I locked into the superpower of perception alteration. Once I adopted this mindset, I was free as a bird. The Art of the Shoulder Shrug is real and highly effective. If you haven't tried it, I strongly suggest you give it a whirl. I am becoming increasingly skilled at dwelling in the space of "unbothered." Whatever you cannot change, make peace with it, and follow Elsa's lead and let that stuff go. It is so much easier said than done, especially when you feel slighted and injured. But trust me when I say that the victory you feel when you forgive and move on is indescribable.

There is now a renewed intentionality concerning my thoughts and inner conversations. I whip empowering thoughts from my toolbelt as soon as negative ones try to creep in. I channel my inner Mary J. Blige whenever something feels "off," reminding myself that it's "Just Fine." I work diligently to combat any deleterious activity or energy in my midst. I have begun studying energy and vibrations. I am not playing around. Peace is my right and I want all of it!

Again, I am ecstatic to disclose that I did not, and could not, do this alone. The village came and helped drag me out of the quicksand. Every day, all day, I am bombarded with reminders of my "why." Thoughtful and uplifting souvenirs of my inner strength and beauty come in the form of inspirational words, songs, and pictures when I need them most. My lovely daughter created an in-home self-care facility in her home. An amazing and talented sorority sister fashioned a wonderful spot in her home for me and treated me like a queen! I have felt strong love energy radiating from near and far. The village has poured into, checked on, supported, and taken a chance on me during one of the most challenging periods of my life.

Before concluding this session, I am obligated to share the lessons I have learned about love and friendship. This is important because without it, re-stabilizing my mind would have been exceedingly difficult. Iconic superstar Michael Jackson sang one of my favorite take-aways from this transformation experience, "I've learned that love is not possession." Michael may have been referring to romantic love, but I am talking about ALL kinds of pure love. I understand now that when someone loves you, they want what's best for you. It does not keep a tally of what it does for you so it can send you a "bill." It wants to give you peace and serenity. It demands of you to be and do your best. It wants you to be okay and will do "whatever it takes to get you there." It also forgives and extends grace. There was a time when I blocked love because some who claimed to hold it for me almost destroyed me. Now, I am a champion for it. What tore me down has rebuilt me!

Compliments and kind, encouraging words have also been mac and cheese and collard greens for my soul during this difficult, yet prolific time in my life. I saw a meme somewhere that read "Compliments will only take you so far." I agree with this statement, but there is something I would like to add here. When my ascension process began the FIRST-time years ago, I was at a low point. Overnight I had gone from beautiful and in shape to overweight with my hair suddenly turning grey. I did NOT feel great about myself. I worked so hard to further educate myself, remain fit and healthy, and take diligent care of my children. But life happened and threw me totally off my square.

Recently, at the inception of this ascension go-around, I found myself in a similar space. I was mentally, physically, and spiritually exhausted. My hair and skin were being insolent and insubordinate, and my mind said, "Screw this!" and left. The reasons for this will be discussed in a future publication, but the crucial point is that genuine compliments gave me vitamins and minerals I needed to begin again. Compliments are things I gave by the boatload because I was aware of how they made people feel. I am nothing close to a saint, so my mouth has uttered things my mother would be extremely disappointed to hear, but I try to make people feel good as much as possible.

Uplifting words in the form of compliments put a smile on my face. They caused me to shift the focus back to myself when necessary. It is true that compliments only take you so far, as consistent effort and action carry you the rest of the way. I get that. What compliments do for the spirit is what I am speaking on. They boost confidence when someone is experiencing self-esteem and self-image challenges. They foster courage to try more and be more when you doubt yourself and your abilities. They let you know that you are not invisible. A compliment can be the difference between someone choosing to take his or her life or remaining with us. I know this because a drive-thru window worker confided in me a couple of years ago that my compliment made him second guess a suicide attempt. For these reasons, I will continue to give compliments whenever I can.

I am currently doing research regarding how trauma affects the memory. I cannot at this time recall many of the details of the last 18 months of my life, but I can parlay the experience into a single statement. There is a phenomenal quote by our beloved Dr. Maya Angelou that says, "People will forget what you said, people will forget what you did, but people will never forget how you made them feel." I feel all of that! I want to use this portion of this chapter to thank every unselfish, magnificent soul who made me feel loved, safe, and secure as I continue to flap my wings. Because you poured into me, I have the strength to continue to evolve and pour into others. Everybody wins!

F*uel* for F*light*

I pray that you can see and feel the light that I am sending out to you right now. You possess an unlimited capacity to shift your perspective and focus. Cloudy thoughts will come, that's part of the human experience. What makes you amazing is that you possess the tools and skills to clear a path for the sun to come out and light up in your mind. Never underestimate the power of your default status, nor your ability to create and re-create what you desire it to be. Keep focusing on the blessings in your lessons. This is where the wind will lift you into the air!

Shift

Your

Environment

Environment:

the conditions, surroundings, and influences that affect the health, growth, and progress of a person

W*hat?*

Friends, environment is an extremely integral part of any healing process. In it is everything you are exposed to. What you see, hear, taste, smell, all of these make up your environment. Added to these are the people, places, and situations that make up our everyday lives. Another critical part is the overall general tone of the atmosphere where you spend your time. If you are a happy-go-lucky person with a lighthearted zest for life, you may not fair well in an environment absent of light and love. For example, along my journey I have always been a lover of music and the arts. Singing, dancing, and most music styles are a must-have for my emotional thermostat to be raised. I do not do well in oppressive, rigid environments. Because of this, you will likely find me in the presence of some sort of music most of my waking hours.

W*hy?*

For my Phoenixes who happen to be parents, have you ever found yourself telling your babies to turn off the TV or the music while studying? Why do you do that? To minimize distractions and provide the best possible conditions for success. As an adult, you know that noise pulls the focus away from the business at hand, interfering with progress. The same principle applies to your ascension. Excessive background noise will keep you permanently rolling around in the dirty ashes screaming, "I've fallen, and I can't get up!" Noise is heavy. Its gravity will keep you grounded instead of in flight where you belong.

H*ow?* (Reflect, Assign, Adjust)

Shifting your environment may mean shifting things and people OUT of it completely. There are things that simply don't make sense for where your ascension is taking you. These choices are sometimes difficult and heartbreaking. In specific cases, a repositioning will be more appropriate. Reflect on your "why" and fortify it. Make sure it's strong enough to endure the backlash and discomfort of atmospheric change and pressure. The higher you go, the more people will fall off, and the lonelier it gets. Just know that you won't be up there by yourself for long. There are other people ready to soar!

Should you choose to the removal route, it does not mean that the absence must be permanent. Sometimes the position of people in our lives *is* the adjustment. In my own life, there are people who have transitioned out but are irreplaceable and for whom my love is endless. On the other hand, I have made new acquaintances who have enriched my life massively. Some new acquaintances are old acquaintances who have re-emerged and taken a different seat. Regardless of the circumstance, the sincere and honest presence of people in our lives are a gift. The gift comes in and for varied reasons and seasons. The key is to be grateful for the gift.

ℵ **Reflect:** When my most recent ascension phase began, I took a moment to reflect on every aspect of my atmosphere. I pondered what was working and what wasn't. Where and how was I spending my time and with whom? There was an honest, tough inner conversation about what I was doing to sabotage myself. I also had to take a close look at how I could have been sabotaging others. This part of the process was difficult because it meant letting go of things that I did not want to release. There were habits that I *thought* I liked. Yes, this part made me skittish.

ℵ **Assign:** After careful reflection, there was a need to re-assign placement. This meant reprioritizing my time, effort, and energy. In short, I had to stop

majoring in the minors and begin putting first things
first.

- א **Adjust:** Finally, the actual adjustments were put into
  place. Again, this is a learned skill that I am
  improving daily. For example, I am more mindful of
  the nature and timing of communications. I
  rearranged my physical space to make it more
  conducive to achieving my goals and objectives.

If you need some ideas for switching things up, I offer these
suggestions:

- **Physical Environment**: You could try adding plants
  or other greenery to your home or office. Incense,
  candles, and other "smell goods" release endorphins
  that lift the mood. They do it for me every time.
  Photos of loved ones, paintings, and wall decals add a
  nice touch and remind you of your "why."
  Rearranging furniture for a fresh look can provide a
  sense of newness to your space.

- **Spiritual Environment**: Prayer and inspirational
  messages have done wonders for me. Protecting the
  spirit is critical! Your spirit houses your intuition.
  Trust it. If something doesn't feel right, feel free to
  respond accordingly. I am still a work in progress
  with this one. I endeavor to improve daily.

- **Mental/Emotional Environment**: It was not until
  recently that peace became non-negotiable. Anything
  that causes mental, emotional, or spiritual imbalance
  must go. I have had to do this numerous times during
  my ascension phase, especially when my feet were
  still low to the ground. I keep my light givers close.

Each day brings more healing and sensitivity to what I see and hear. Positivity is always the goal.

Transformational Transparency

I could author an entire book about the effects of environment on ascension alone. Due to circumstances beyond my control, and some within, my BS detector was non-functional for much of my life. You could sell me tickets to a Superbowl game in July and I would give you the money and start getting ready. Good grief! I was much too trusting, of too many people, far too quickly. This was a trait that as a youngster, loved ones repeatedly tried to tell me would be my undoing. It was, and it costed me dearly.

In fact, I did not realize that it mattered. I was too busy always slaying those darn dragons to even detect that my physical, spiritual, and mental atmosphere were out of order and misaligned. Honey, there was a time when I was everywhere, doing everything, with everybody. It was ALL wrong! There were no boundaries because mine were forcibly crossed so many times that I eventually just opened the borders. This is the tragic consequence of trauma.

Now, allow me to introduce you to besties grace, favor, and mercy. When those borders were opened, riffraff slid on through between the gates, but so did my angels. In case you didn't know, angels DO exist, and I am using this platform to attest to that fact. This is my story and I'm sticking to it. My angels in human form walked with me through the worst times of my life. I didn't realize it until recently, after I submitted to isolation and created a space of quiet and reflection. From elementary school until this very day, my angels have stood watch over me, praying, pouring, loving, and protecting. None of them have shown me their wings, but I have always sensed their presence.

My angels had their work cut out for them as I approached my "rock bottom" moment. I am fairly sure they could see it coming and did a full dispatch of all available personnel. Thank goodness they sent their best, most highly trained out to cover the scene of my pre-pandemic breakdown on a two-lane highway. That narrow brush with death sent a loud and clear message that said,

> "My angels had their work cut out for them as I approached my "rock bottom" moment."

"Look, Lady. Get your mind right or you won't have to worry about it because you won't be here." Roger that, sir! Sometimes that's what it takes to get our attention and call us to action.

That call to action led to drastic changes over a stretch of time. My healing and soaring process has not been linear. I have backtracked and backpedaled, flying high, then crashing and burning, and I'm fine with it. No experience is wasted in this life, and my crashes were no exception. Every plummet to the Earth, though painful and disappointing, was calorie and nutrient dense with food for my next flight. The meal had to be consumed to reap the benefits. I did not always like the taste of the "lesson meals," but they were good for me.

These meals were high in Vitamin K because they sharpened my vision. Revelations regarding my daily interactions were soon undeniable. I was spending exorbitant amounts of time on things that were not pushing me into the highest realm of purpose. I was creating and engaging in activities that were purposeful, however, the execution needed upgrading. My heart, mind, and spirit were aligned and my intentions pure, but my atmosphere was stunting my growth. Words needed to change, relationships needed to be altered, and my mindset needed an overhaul. These crucial factors can make or break purpose-fulfillment.

The spice in this soup is that there really was no choice except to adjust my surroundings. My perceived "superhero" calling, stress created by my own trauma management, as well as the occasional Jack in the Box left on my doorstep, generated a vibration that reverberated problems, issues, and dysfunction. Instead of sending this energy back to the sender, I invited it in, sat down, and had tea and scones. I'm sure you can envision it. It was like having a pocket full of lint trying to loan someone $20.

Then one day the train came to a screeching halt. The brake lever was pulled all the way back. Enough was enough. My brain needed a reprieve from all the activity. I couldn't necessarily see it but someone outside of me could. The filter was full to the max and could not manage another iota of negativity. Managing the past, present, and future all at once had worn me out mentally, physically, and spiritually. The time had arrived to stop allowing my actions to betray my words, as the great motivational speaker Inky Johnson so often says. I had a pocket full of money earned from all the wolf tickets I sold declaring each day was THE day that I cut off dysfunction and drama.

Honestly speaking, it was extremely hard at first because it meant detaching from energy that had been long been present in my life. It felt counter-intuitive. Habits and steel are a challenge to break. Negativity is habit forming. Negative talk and behaviors release addictive chemicals in the brain the same as when we engage in positivity. Making pivotal changes to central aspects of environment had a significantly constructive impact on all areas of my health. As a result, my children have benefited from the adjust- ments that I submitted to in my life.

F*uel* for F*light*

Changes to your environment can be scary and unsettling, especially when it comes to moving people around within that framework. Sometimes folks get upset and don't understand. You may hesitate, but your self-awareness whispers quietly that it's what will serve you best. Know that you have the right and duty to create the most conducive setting for your ascension. Believe that when all is said and done, decisions made from a clean heart will always produce phenomenal results.

Unweight

Your

Wings

Weight:

To hold something down by placing a heavy object on top of it.

What?

This chapter will be short, sweet, and to the point. Trying to fly with your wings weighted down is futile. I tried it for decades and believe me, it does not work out well. I know that you are an unselfish, loving, giving empath who lives for assisting others in their struggles. I love that! I just do not want you to compromise your mental health to do it. The world needs people who assist one another along life's journey, and I want you to remain healthy, happy, and whole while doing so.

Why?

The primary reason for my breakdown on that two-lane highway was the massive load I was carrying in my mind and spirit. My propensity to hold on to the past, to control the present, and protect the future came at a considerable price. Those dragons would not stay down. They resented feeling defeated, so they made certain to continue making periodic appearances so I wouldn't forget them (the devastating effects of their presence was not sufficient to achieve this goal). I constantly refer to this event because it marked the beginning of my first ascension phase. This phase was the earliest brick on the road to lasting change.

I no longer wished to live this way, but I had to put in the work to change the narrative. Other people were being adversely affected and it needed to change. There were multiple reasons why I became vested in lightening my load:

- **To protect my peace**
- **To remain focused on the obligations and responsibilities that matter most**
- **To maintain my mental, physical, and spiritual health**

ℵ **To create the most optimal environment for my success**

H*ow?*

My eldest daughter pointed out that people in need are drawn to people who help. I am a helper and a fixer. It is a natural element of my character, which was passed down through my maternal lineage. Growing up I watched my grandmother share with complete strangers when she had almost nothing to give. My mother will give a person in need her last if it means that individual's life will be blessed. My daughter is the same way. Wherever we see suffering it is our first inclination to relieve it. It's just how we're wired. We've never done so from a selfish or attention-seeking place, but from a genuine heart.

The method I used to unweight my wings was simple. I started minding my own business and leaving other folks' business alone. I will always be willing and ready to lend a helping hand, but I am more aware of how and when I do it. I retired the superhero cape, choosing to concentrate on growing and developing myself and those I love. This one hurt, because at a point my identity had become encapsulated in martyring myself for the good of the order. The trip to Breakdownsville taught me that line of thinking was out of order. What started as a willing offering slowly turned into a burnt sacrifice. I am pleased to report that I have since jumped off the alter and into flight mode! In doing so, it snatched others off the alter as well.

As I penned in a poem recently, I am a human hope supply, but I supply that hope differently now. I do what I can when I can. My purpose and assignment have not changed; however, my focal point has. As I soar higher, and heal more extensively, I am certain that the universe will reveal to me the appropriate manner of dispensation. Until then, I will persist in focusing acutely on myself and my personal responsibilities.

There is another relevant message that I cannot in good conscience leave out of this section. To free yourself and stop carrying extra weight around is to SPEAK YOUR TRUTH! I cannot emphasize enough how vital this is for your mind, spirit, soul, and heart. Speak it! Say it! Own it! You may face opposition and backlash, but you will also find support in the most unexpected places. As the recording artist Jon Mayer so eloquently put it, "Say what you need to say." Boldly and apologetically tell your story and speak your speech. I can attest that not doing so places an unbearable weight on your wings, rendering your flight almost impossible. You are strong and brave! Speak!

> "SPEAK YOUR TRUTH"

Transformational Transparency

I am still a work in progress in this area, but I am making considerable strides daily. My tendencies and desires to support and pour into others are as strong as ever. The difference now is that I am selective about who, what, when, where, why, and how I support, if I step in at all. I am no longer willing to sacrifice my family. I am learning to accept assistance when needed. I do not regret a single smile, empowering and uplifting exchange, or minutes that I offered with a pure heart. I simply returned what the universe gave me when I needed it most. I fully comprehend that it is not my responsibility to save the world. It never was. That is the Creator's job. My task is to bring love and light wherever I place my feet, using the small, still voice inside of me as a guide.

F*uel* for F*light*

I can only fathom how liberating and exhilarating flying must be for a bird. Feeling the wind lift you higher and higher must be a major rush. That is the feeling you encounter when you unburden yourself and permit unrestricted flight. You deserve to be light and lively; to live unapologetically for you and those you love. There is no insolence or shame in focusing on you.

Fly

In

Faith

Faith:

Something that is believed, especially with strong conviction.

W *hat?*

Stop and look around. No longer are you sitting in the soot and ashes of your previous trip to the sun. You are clean, determined, and prepared for the next step. You have lightened your load, cleared a path, and mastered your mind. Standing in an upright position, head pointed up and wings spread wide, the moment is drawing closer. With intensity mounting and adrenaline pumping through your magnificent body, there is a poignant question that only you can answer: Do you have the faith that it takes to leave the ground?

Risk: No action forces the universe to up the ante like a risk move. When you take a risk, you make an investment with no guarantee of a return. You are agreeing to give up something, not knowing if you will ever get anything back. Just like in Vegas, you can risk a little, or you can risk a lot. It all depends on your level of belief, and what value you attach to it. Faith thrives on your willingness to take a risk to receive a reward. This has not been easy for me, but I know it will yield sweet fruit in the end.

Notice the word "believed" in the definition of faith. The word believe means that you accept is true or real. Faith does not exist without belief. They are conjoined like Siamese twins. You must **believe** that you can soar. You must **believe** that your worst days are behind you. You must **believe** that you will reap the harvest of your pain sown in tears and frustration. You must **believe** that the investments you made by staying the course and pushing through the pain will yield unfathomable dividends. You must **believe** that this is your time to rise!

W*hy?*

Why is faith necessary for a successful rising? Because without it nothing happens. When you sink in the quicksand of doubt and uncertainty, and you feel that your will is not strong enough to see you through, faith will come in and shut all of that down. When you have faith, the universe has no choice but to move on your behalf. The great motivational speaker Billy Alsbrooks stated it well when he said, "Destiny is obligated by universal law to yield to the demands of unwavering faith." Think about the power that lies in believing in something that there is yet any evidence of. There's nothing like it.

In the Bible faith enabled Peter to walk on water. Faith told the Wright Brothers that the airplane was attainable. Faith sustained enslaved Africans all over the globe through one of the worst atrocities in human history. Faith nestles the minds and spirits of people battling life-threatening illnesses, whispering healing and hope in their ears. Faith will feed you when you are starving for something to hold on to. Faith is your secret weapon!

H*ow?* (Action, Risk, Planning)

Faith is such an abstract concept that it is tricky to explain how to use it. Instead, I will share from my experience what it takes to make it work: activation. Faith **MUST** be activated if it is to be useful. This is non-negotiable. What does activation entail? I'm so glad you asked.

- **Action:** Faith thrives on actions. When you profess to have faith, the universe is going to ask pivotal questions: What have you done to prove your faith? What actionable steps have you taken toward what you say that you want to achieve? What have you done to show that you hold the belief that you claim to have? In case you haven't heard faith without works is dead, and you don't want anything dead in your atmosphere.

‏ℵ‎ **Risk:** No action forces the universe to up the ante like a risk move. When you take a risk, you make an investment with no guarantee of a return. You are agreeing to give up something, not knowing if it will ever get anything back. Just like in Vegas, you can risk a little, or you can risk a lot. It all depends on your level of belief. Faith thrives on your willingness to take a risk to receive a reward.

‏ℵ‎ **Planning:** "Faith was never meant to be passive. You must be aggressive even in the waiting." This quote that I heard on a podcast perfectly articulates my stance on this step. Faith requires patience. There is a waiting period between the believing and the blessing. The universe will honor a plan created to arrive at your intended destination. Planning triggers the universe into movement because it is an indication that you are serious.

Transformational Transparency

This section will be brief. There is no way I would have gotten an inch off the ground without faith. Not one millimeter. But it was not entirely *my* faith that got the job done. It was other people's faith in me that carried me when I had little to none in myself. This is the seed that I want to plant way down in the soil of your spirit. Sometimes you won't have the faith, and that's alright. Life's disappointments and challenges have a way of disintegrating what little belief we may have. That's why the village is so important. Folks outside of you can see from a bird's eye point of view what you cannot see up close.

In my case, I had more faith in others than I did in myself. Yes, that's one of the brightly wrapped gifts that trauma leaves in your birthday basket. When you are mishandled, misused, or abused in any way, it skews the way you view yourself and your value. This is particularly true if there have been multiple incidents or prolonged exposure to challenging circumstances. Not only do you blame yourself, but you no longer trust your own judgement. Your faith is placed in jeopardy because it becomes difficult to believe in what you *do* see, let alone what you cannot.

Then one day, there was a spark, a tiny flame that glinted in the darkness. That spark came in the form of a school nurse, school psychologist, and school social workers employed by the district I worked in as a teacher's assistant. I will never forget those life-giving, faith-building words spoken over me that cold, winter day. As a collective they said, "We have been watching you for some time now, and you have a tremendous gift. This place is too small for you. It is time to move on. We don't want to see you back here next year." That pierced my spirit and blew my mind. The next month I enrolled into graduate school and began a master's program in teaching. That actionable step set it off!

> "Then one day, there was a spark, a tiny flame that glinted in the darkness."

Another example of a surrogate faith moment was born with the publishing of my first book. I had been talking about drafting a book for years but had no real faith that I could do it. It seemed unreachable and impossible. It felt like a pipe dream. Until the day my dear sorority sister challenged me with these words, "Big Sissy, you have so much to share. Just go ahead and write your book and I'll publish it!" Another faith-borrowing moment occurred when a sister-friend called and asked me what I was doing on a lazy Saturday afternoon. "Just reading," I said. Her next statement gut punched me. "Are you the author of that book? Why aren't you reading your own book?" Microphone drop moment of the century! My first two books were published within the next 8 months.

There is a myriad of faith moments that I could share with you, but suffice is to say that without action, risk, and planning, there would be no story to tell. As Bishop TD Jakes so eloquently put it, "Sometimes you have to believe in someone else's belief in you until yours kicks in." I had to this, and so will you at some point. Take comfort in knowing that eventually, yours WILL kick in. Act now! No step is too large or too small. There is an old Chinese proverb that says, "The journey of 1,000 miles begins with one small step." Have faith. Take the step. You are worth it!

F*uel* for F*light*

Aside from love, faith is the most powerful force on the planet. The willingness to believe in something that has not taken place is nothing short of remarkable. It is saying yes when all around you looks like no. Faith sharpens your vision of the future and propels you toward destiny. It takes you to an untouchable place inside of yourself. Consistent and unwavering faith makes you unstoppable! Activate your faith. Take the risk and get your reward!

Arise:

to move upward.

I can hear the wildly talented R&B group Boys II Men singing, "although we've come to the end of the road…" The road to ascension has been long and hard. You have been a warrior throughout this process! Slaying dragons, bringing your thoughts under submission, falling in love with yourself, and fortifying your faith have built the perfect platform for your lift off. It is the end of one era, and the beginning of another, far greater one for both of us. Now that you have done the work, your wings will ceremoniously be set ablaze. Be proud of you! I am proud of you!

Take a moment to envision yourself taking flight. I want you to really go there in your mind. Sense the moment your feet leave the ground. Picture the ashes where you once slept appearing increasingly smaller as you fly higher toward your life source. Imagine the intensity of the exhilaration. Allow pure, concentrated joy, freedom, and power to simultaneously flood your mind and spirit. Smile, laugh, and cry, or yell with delight as you intake the sheer magnitude of the moment. Liberation is at hand! You are airborne! Phoenix, you have ascended!

How does it feel? Sit in it. Let the moment overtake you. Breathe it in. No matter the length of your journey, you made it. Give yourself proper credit for the dedication that you have shown to your healing and forward movement. The incredible work you have done should not be taken lightly. Hercules, you were brave enough to attempt an improbable feat. Celebrate that and celebrate you. Remember to always extend to yourself the same grace, compassion, understanding, and love that you afford others. You matter! You are important! You are irreplaceable!

Rise, Phoenix, Rise!

Prologue

The transcendence and transformation of the Phoenix never occurs in a straight line. There are zig zags, loops and turns, rises and falls. As stated in the introduction, it is not about perfection. Ascension does not carry with it the assumption of flawlessness. I do not believe that anyone ever achieves that. The great transformational change for me was about getting up out of the dirt, washing my face, and having the courage to try again. It was not easy. In fact, this ascension attempt was the most challenging to date. Shame, fear, and total vulnerability were all part of the equation. There was a point when I was required to depend solely on those around me to keep me safe and protected. I reverted to an infancy state against my own will, not fully comprehending what my will truly was. Indeed, I was forced to walk by faith and not by sight.

The transforming of the Phoenix, the rise from ashes to ascension, is not complete. I am not sure if it ever is. Soaring and kissing the sun is only the beginning for me. The ascension is not for me to remain suspended in the air as a spectacle for all to see. The momentous change, the chaos, and the struggle are for the benefit of those who need my light and heat. It is for the building of legacy. Most importantly, the ascension is the Herculean impossible feat I thought I could never perform. Now, the real work begins...

About the Author

LESA BUTLER is an author, educator, and speaker originally from Chicago, Illinois. Lesa is the author of "What If," "From the Depths of My Soul," and "Phoenix Transforming." She is the CEO of Divine Reimaging, LLC, and founder and president of Woman, Discover Thyself, a women's empowerment non-profit organization. Lesa holds a degree in Justice Systems, a Master of Arts in Teaching, and completed post-graduate study in Community Counseling. She has created children's entrepreneurship programs such as The Youth Entrepreneurship Bootcamp and New Legacy Academy, an educational experience designed to empower youth to use their gifts and talents to create economic opportunities. Lesa is the mother of three exceptional children. When she is not hammering away at a project, she can be found traveling, writing, and dancing.

Lesa Butler

Thank you for sharing this journey with me!
I would love to know your thoughts.
Please send a review to:

authorlesab@gmail.com
and/or
Lesa Butler - S.H.E. PUBLISHING, LLC
(shepublishingllc.com)

Are you ready to make your next event
TRANSFORMATIONAL?
Book me for:

- Speaking Engagements
- Writing & Authorship Workshops
- Book Development Projects
- Ghostwriting

www.ingramcontent.com/pod-product-compliance
Lightning Source LLC
Chambersburg PA
CBHW040902120626
46551CB00001B/132